The
Alan Clark Diaries:
Thatcher's Fall

A PHOENIX PAPERBACK

This abridged edition, published in 1996 by Phoenix, contains pages
edited by the author from
Diaries by Alan Clark

First published in Great Britain by
Weidenfeld & Nicolson in 1993
A paperback edition published in 1994 by Phoenix,
A division of Orion Books Ltd,
Orion House, 5 Upper St Martin's Lane, London WC2H 9EA

Cover illustration: Margaret Thatcher at the Conservative Party
conference in 1985; © Hulton Deutsch collection

ISBN: 1 85799 529 5

Typeset by Selwood Systems, Midsomer Norton

Printed in Great Britain by Clays Ltd, St Ives plc

Alan Clark writes:

Although at the time it seemed sudden, and surprising, the fall of Margaret Thatcher was a long-drawn out affair and, I find, there are many traces of its approach in my Diaries for 1990 and indeed in 1989.

From the full published edition I have selected a number of entries, excising those that did not apply.

The sequence starts with a reference to a (failed) pre-emptive strike by the Thatcher camp.

Saltwood   *Saturday, 3 March*

A little dinner at Lyall Street.[1] Just Aspers, Jimmy Goldsmith and Charles Powell. The 'guest' was Conrad Black,[2] the purpose to see to what extent he was amenable to being leant on, in the gentlest manner of course, to steer Max[3] away from plugging Heseltine so much. The answer, it soon became clear, was – not at all.

Black is young, quite attractive looking, very clever and widely read. If I look back over the newspaper tycoons I've known it is only Beaverbrook with whom he compares. Some are just thick, others like Roy Thomson bluff away and you don't know, but they're boring. Cap'n Bob is the most entertaining, I suppose, but you never quite feel he's giving you his full *attention* – and this for reasons, let's say, unrelated to the setting in which the conversation is taking place.

The subject had to be approached delicately. Charles was diplomatic, Jimmy blunt. But Black simply couldn't care. He made a competent, almost dismissive defence.

[1] Number 1, Lyall Street, town house of John Aspinall.
[2] Conrad Black, Canadian newspaper proprietor, born 1944, who had come to London and bought the *Daily Telegraph* in 1987.
[3] Max Hastings, Editor of the *Daily Telegraph* since 1986.

It's my paper, I do what I think right, anyway he (Heseltine)
is an interesting chap, we look like we're in a mess, heading
for a bigger one, etc.

Black's preference seemed to be for talking about Wash-
ington. He's knowledgeable and interesting here too. But
as to its principal objective, the dinner was a failure.

Saltwood   *Sunday, 4 March*

A beautiful day of early spring, quite perfect in light,
colour, the shadow and tone of stone and lawn and
blossom. We have started to mow with the sit-down
mowers that roll and stripe. No more rotaries until Sep-
tember when the plantains grow.

I was resigned to settling back 'with the Heritage' when
I had a long call from Tristan which electrified me.[4]

We're 28 points behind in the polls, and the leadership
is in a panic. The Lady has rocky moments of self doubt.
(This has happened before, I told him, Carol used to tell me
how dejected she became in 1985 when all the economic
indicators were looking good but people still wouldn't
respond.) The Cabinet are all over the place. Most of them
are 'pretty doubtful about' (read *loathe*) her but don't
know what to do. G. Howe is behaving 'poorly', *chétif*
and unsupportive. The Government have got to find a

---

[4]Tristan Garel-Jones had been Deputy Chief Whip since 1989.

billion, at once, to buy off the Poll Tax complainants.

'That won't be enough,' I sniggered.

House of Commons   *Wednesday, 28 March*

The Lady is under deep pressure now. It just won't go away. As soon as one paper goes quiet another one, or two at a time, start up.

As far as I can make out practically every member of the Cabinet is quietly and unattributably briefing different Editors or members of the Lobby about how awful she is. This makes it easier for people like Peter Jenkins[5] to say that 'she has virtually lost all support in Cabinet'. Malcolm Rifkind[6] is actually quoted today as saying, 'I'll be here after she's gone.'

There is even talk of a coup in July. Heseltine is quite openly spoken about as the heir-presumptive, and preens himself in public.

How has all this been allowed to come about? The Community Charge has got on everyone's nerves of course, and generated the most oppressive volume of correspondence. Persistent deficits in the polls of a nearly insuperable order rattle people. But I am inclined to think that the Party in the House has just got sick of her.

[5]Political columnist on *The Independent*.
[6]Malcolm Rifkind, MP for Edinburgh Pentlands since 1974. Secretary of State for Scotland since 1986.

She hasn't promoted her 'own' people much. Her
'constituency' in this place depends solely on her proven
ability to win General Elections. But now this is in jeop-
ardy she has no real Praetorian Guard to fall back on.
There's been a lot of talk about 'one of us', all that, but
most of them are still left to moulder at the '92 dinner
table. When's the Revolution? In the meantime, all the
wets and Blue Chips and general Heathite wankers, who
seem ineradicable in this bloody Party, stew around and
pine for her to drop dead.

Most critics move, in the open, under (pretty
transparent) camouflage. A number of 'heavy' back-
benchers of the 'Centre' (i.e. Left) of the Party have let it
be known that her 'Decision-making Circle' should be
widened, that they are uneasy about the 'privileged access'
enjoyed by 'certain key and unelected advisors'.

This of course is a shot across the bows for Charles
[Powell] and Bernard [Ingham]. But without them she
really would be lost, as the Chief Whip, Tim Renton, is
Howe's creature; Peter Morrison is of little use as a PPS
under these conditions; Gow is neutered and doesn't cut
ice any longer.

House of Commons   *Monday, 2 April*

Last night there were riots in Central London – just like
1981. All the anarchist scum, class-war, random drop-

outs and trouble-seekers had infiltrated the march and started beating up the police.[7]

There is this strain in most Western countries (except, curiously, the United States) but it is particularly prevalent in Britain, where this rabble have – confirming their middle-class social origins – their own press in *The Grauniad* and *The Independent*. Far from having their capers cut by the revolution in Russia, the removal of a distant but supportive ideological menace, they are flourishing in that very curtailment of discipline and order which the fall of the ancient Soviet autocracy has brought about.

But it is bad. *Civil Disorder.* Could cut either way, but I fear will scare people into wanting a compromise – just as did Saltley Colliery and the three-day week in 1972/3. In the corridors and the tea room people are now talking openly of ditching the Lady to save their skins. This is the first time I've heard it *en clair* since a bad patch (1977?) when we were in opposition. Some of the Lobby, Tony Bevins[8] in particular, hang around outside the Members' post office and fly kites.

There is a wild rumour going round that she may be 'deputised' at the end of July. 'Uh? Deputised?'

'Yes, you know, receive a deputation, the Chief Whip,

---

[7] An anti-poll tax demonstration in central London.
[8] Anthony Bevins, Political Editor of *The Independent*. His father, Reginald, had been an MP, and Postmaster-General, 1959–64.

the '22 Executive, Willie, that kind of thing. Told to throw in the towel.'

Contemptible.

Ministry of Defence   *Thursday, 5 April*

The Lady scowled startledly at me on Tuesday when she came in for Questions. Although she is completely absorbed in her own brief, hyped to the nines for her ordeal against little Kinnock, and pays no attention to her surroundings whatever, her presence beside one on the bench is always a little constraining.

The Last Days[9] and the Whips are divided among themselves. Some want blood. Some, covertly, want 'a change'. G-J's own position is equivocal and he probably thinks, may even have been told, that Heseltine would make him Chief. Renton, the existing Chief, doesn't think strategically – or even tactically. He is amiable, social; but never did his groundwork as a junior in 'the office'. In any case, my suspicion has always been that his loyalties incline towards Geoffrey Howe.

Gow, Ryder, Aitken and I dined at 'Greens' the 'new' restaurant on Locketts' old site, set up under the aegis of Simon Parker Bowles (*relation*, I assume). Confirmed the bad impression when Alison and I tried it out last week.

[9] *The Last Days of Hitler* by Hugh Trevor-Roper, AC's tutor at Oxford, now Lord Dacre.

Waiters either *completely* incapable of understanding English – or French, or Italian. Are they Rumanians from an AIDS hostel? – or chinless youths, spaced-outly smiling and chatting to each other in upper-class accents, waiting to get on the waiting list (sic) for Cirencester.

The boys were gloomy. We none of us see our way. Quite difficult to approach the Lady at the moment, as Ian is finding. And what advice do we give her? Shed blood, I said.

Saltwood   *Friday, 20 April*

A date which usually marks a period of good fortune. Yesterday evening Tristan and I repaired to Wilton's. Tristan has written a paper in his own hand; circulated it to the Chief Whip, Ingham (?!), Andrew Turnbull,[10] John Major and Mark Lennox-Boyd.[11]

Not, I noted, to Charles. No point, he said, CP 'too fanatically committed'.

Each of the recipients had 'tried to push him through her door' (i.e. to say it in person).

'Well, why don't you?'

Yes, he was going to supper at the Number 10 flat on

[10] Andrew Turnbull, Principal Private Secretary to the PM.
[11] Mark Lennox-Boyd, MP for Morecambe since 1979. Parliamentary Private Secretary to the Prime Minister since 1988.

Sunday – just him and X-B[12] – and told me how he proposed to play it. The Party was 'lazy, sullen, and frightened'. Unless there was a marked improvement by early to mid-October *over* 100 votes would be cast against her at the leadership contest, which was inevitable, in the month following. Tristan's view was that over 100 against would mean that she would have to stand down.

I couldn't help grinning. 'Try telling her that.'

Tristan named a number of individuals (ranging from Phil Goodhart[13] to Marlow[14]) who were totally disillusioned, didn't bother to vote any longer. Party discipline was breaking up. All this he would say if necessary.

It is clear, although he didn't say as much, that he has a low opinion of Renton, who has not got a grip on things. In any case, Renton is Geoffrey's nominee, has no feelings towards the Lady.

I said that 'Mid October' was balls. The time scale was far shorter. It had to be settled before the Party Conference and that meant, effectively, in *this* parliamentary term – which in turn means before 15 July, because for those last two weeks of the Summer Term we are all in a limbo of rumour, lassitude and low motivation. Proper

[12]X-B: AC here uses the abbreviation employed by Jim Lees-Milne when referring to Mark's father, Alan (later 1st Viscount Boyd of Merton), Colonial Secretary, 1954–9.
[13]Philip Goodhart, MP for Beckenham since 1957.
[14]Tony Marlow, MP for Northampton North since 1979.

consideration cannot be given until after the May local election results have been analysed, so that means that the *band* stretches from mid-May until mid-July, no more.

At this exact point in our conversation I spotted Heseltine coming up the steps from the bar! And with Mates![15] He was shown, not to a nearby, but to the *adjoining* table. This was ludicrous. He and Mates sat down, got up again immediately, were spirited away.

A nearby group of 'businessmen' were oggly. 'Didn't take long to get rid of *him*,' I said, without reverence.

But I bet Michael was thinking, 'They won't treat me like that when I'm Prime Minister.' One more score to settle with Clark. A little later I signalled to Albert [head waiter] and said would he please give Mr Heseltine my compliments and apologies for spoiling his evening. I would be very glad if he would allow me to settle his bill.

But whether Albert did so or not, I don't know. If he did, the offer was not accepted.

House of Commons   *Tuesday, 1 May*

I had a conversation with IG in the smoking room. Aitken joined us. What could we do to succour the Lady? Do we even want to? We were stuck with the same inflation rate as when we came into power in 1979. Ten, eleven years of endeavour (or however we call all those deprivations

[15]Michael Mates, MP for East Hampshire since 1983.

to life and family) and nothing to show for it but the passage of time and the intrusion of age.

We had moved into the chess room for privacy, but it was dinner time, and posses of MPs moved past on their way through to the dining room, and made mocking comments. Atkins, in particular, is cocky and hostile now, as he watches the decline of the Praetorians.

We came to no conclusions, but aggravated each other's dejection.

Albany   *Monday, 11 June*

To the Gilmours' garden party, at Syon.[16]

The weather was fearfully cold and, as we wandered the gardens, elderly dowagers were complaining of 'frostbite'. Mollie Buccleuch, with a stick (who was it in the Thirties who referred to her and Mary Roxburghe as being 'randy as schoolgirls'?) One of Ian's sons offered to (re)introduce me, and enjoyed it when I said 'no', she disapproved. I told him the story of the Blenheim raid by Loders, in 1950.

[16]Sir Ian Gilmour, 3rd Bt. MP for Chesham since 1974 (Norfolk Central, 1962–74). Former owner of *The Spectator*. Married to Lady Caroline Margaret Montagu-Douglas-Scott, younger daughter of the 8th Duke of Buccleuch.

He was, of course far too young to remember Miss Ball.[17]

People were keen to talk to me, and admiringly curious. I am still in the backwash of the 'Defence Review' publicity.

Young – *policeman* young – Victor Smart[18] came up, after bobbing round a group, and introduced himself. Light-heartedly I protested about his piece: 'There is now considerable doubt as to whether the two Ministers can continue to exist in the same Department', etc.

Then Adam Raphael[19] came up, all ingratiating: 'We're running a Profile of you in the next paper.' After he'd gone Smart said, '*He* was the one who insisted on the 'Two Ministers' bit.'

Willie Whitelaw I also talked to. He was nice, and on the ball and – I was delighted to see – still rheumy-eyed and *repeatedly* calling for his glass to be refilled.

I was hugely cheered by this. If only Willie were still 'around'.

But he is deeply gloomy, in the traditional High Tory way, about electoral prospects. There was a bit of 'does anyone tell her anything?' and 'No good getting mobbed in America, and thinking that's going to work here.'

The fact that Willie no longer has a proper consultative

[17]Miss Ball was a fashionable beautician who had a client list of rich ladies of a certain age, including AC's mother, among whom she used with considerable relish to spread gossip.

[18]Victor Smart, political correspondent, *The Observer*.

[19]Adam Raphael, Executive Editor, *The Observer*, since 1988.

role (in which he was so immensely valuable) is an indict-
ment of our present system of government. He was worked
off his feet as Lord President in order, nominally, to
'justify' his position in Cabinet. He chaired a lot of bloody
stupid committees that easily could have been steered by
any number of different nonentities. In the evenings he
had stuffy dinners, on weekends Party functions.

As a result he got a stroke.

Much better to have been four days a week in Penrith,
and just coming up for Cabinet, and critical meetings.

Albany   *Friday, 20 July*

The last day of 'term', effectively. There is some patchy
business next week, an Opposition supply day on Tuesday,
but nothing to speak of – ending with the Buck House
garden party and a reception at Number 10.

This morning I woke very early, and with that special
late July tranquillity, before even the buses start in Regent
St, and the sky is still pale grey from heat haze. No
shadows as yet, and the promise of another very hot day.

There are few things more delicious than anticipation
of the imminent long summer holiday – particularly
while we still have to taste the picquancy of the 'Junior
Reshuffle'.

Last evening we had the 'End-of-Term Dinner'. Not
quite a dining club, as we only meet on the Thursday

before the Long Recess. There is no actual election process. Membership (and discardment) are osmotic. Ian 'convenes', though Soames and Ryder are each active in organisation. Class is undeniably a factor.

The oval room at White's. Boring food – smoked salmon, roast beef. Who the hell did this, in *July*?

In attendance were Gow, Heathcoat-Amory, Bertie Denham, Jonathan Aitken, Hamilton, Garel-Jones (a 'first' for him!), Alexander Hesketh and Cranborne.[20] Fun to see Robert, and a tribute to IG's discernment as in theory he is out, until 'Harare'[21] dies. But Robert keeps his finger on the pulse, and is knowledgeable.

An uncomfortable atmosphere. We don't like what we see, and we don't like admitting, even to each other, that our beloved leader may be fallible. Not in front of Ian, anyway. But because we don't see our way, substantial political discussion was at a discount. Gossip was stale, and people fell back on dirty stories. Pure dirt, I mean, the Dorm.

I had Soames on my left. 'You'll be in the Cabinet by

[20]David Heathcote-Amory, Parliamentary Under-Secretary, Environment, since 1989; Lord Hesketh, now Minister of State, Trade and Industry. Robert, Viscount Cranborne, heir to the Marquess of Salisbury, had stood down as MP for Dorset South at the 1987 General Election.
[21]6th Marquess of Salisbury.

Monday. Oh no. This is what I hear . . .', etc. He is shameless ('Straight to the Lords'[22]).

A propos of the Lords, was Bertie Denham sounding
me out when he kept asking 'what I wanted'? Was he
trying to lead me into hinting at the Lords as a working
Min of S? Perhaps I muffed it by saying I wanted to be S
of S for Defence. He looked disappointed. He seemed
pretty tight, but the Upper Classes *remember* what they
(and you) say when they were tight.

At the end of the meal, significantly and in contrast to
earlier years, instead of a *tour-de-table* and monologues
on the topics of the day, a colleague's failings, or whatever,
each person gave a little 'performance'.

Ian, *very* boringly, gave us 'Albert and the Lion'. Waste
of time. Bertie was the bluest, Richard the funniest. I did
'Frankie and Johnnie'. Most people know the first few
verses, but the punch line is in the last:

> Sheriff came over in the mornin',
> said it was all for the best.
> He said her lover Johnnie
> was nothin' but a doggone pest.

We don't *need* to have an Election for two years, we
kept telling each other. Technically true, but balls as well.

I thought there would be more talk of a possible 'chal-
lenge' in the autumn but, ominously, there was none. The

---

[22]A phrase in the Clark family signifying a glorious finale.

prospect, though, is implacably in the middle distance. A towering thunderhead of Alto-Cumulus, precursor of change not just in the weather, but in the Climate.

Ministry of Defence   *Monday, 30 July*

I must record a curious phenomenon. If something is happening, or has happened, that affects one adversely, is upsetting – 'bad news' – one feels very tired (over that time) even though one still doesn't know. I remember Jane telling me that she had experienced this on the afternoon we were driving back from Hawtreys and Jason was run over.[23] And this morning I felt dreadful in the Sandling train. It's not just feeling a bit sleepy; it's feeling absolutely shattered, as if one was getting polio, only without the fever.

When I got to the barrier Julian [Scopes] was waiting, looking anxious.

'Minister, I have some very, very bad news.'

For a split second I feared it must be Andrew. But something in his eyes was missing (the look of fear, I suppose, and embarrassment that I might actually *break down*). 'Ian Gow has been killed by a car bomb.'

---

[23] A sad episode in family history when a favourite labrador puppy was killed.

'How spiteful of them', was all I could say. But I thought particularly of the poor Lady. She wept at the first casualties in the Falklands. I wonder if she did today? Because Ian loved her, actually loved, I mean, in every sense but the physical. And then in the end, as lovers do (particularly that kind), he got on her nerves, and she was off-hand with him. He played his last beseeching card: 'I will have to resign.' 'Go ahead, then.' (I foreshorten the exchange, of course) – and that was it.

Saltwood   *Sunday, 4 November*

The papers are all very bad. Tory Party falling apart, the death blow,[24] that kind of thing. Something in it, I fear, unless we can get a grip on events. The only person who can restore order in the parliamentary ranks is Tristan. He can do it short-term (like many intelligent people T. can only see things very long or very short) but that's enough. Get us past November.[25]

---

[24]Sir Geoffrey Howe had resigned from the Government the previous Thursday, and his resignation speech was awaited with some trepidation.
[25]November was the month when under the Leadership Rules, a challenger was permitted to offer himself. Once the month has passed there would be no further opportunity until the new parliamentary session.

After breakfast I telephoned Chequers.

'The Prime Minister is speechwriting.'

'Who with?'

'Charles Powell.'

'When will she be free?'

'There might be a minute before lunch.'

'When's that?'

'One o'clock sharp.'

I was being kept at bay. Unusual. The Number 10 switchboard girls are always helpful. With Chequers I've had this problem before.

'Oh well, please pass her my name, in case she wants to take a call then.'

It was a lovely crisp day of late autumn. I had said I'd join Jane in the garden. Now I was going to be stuck indoors waiting for a call. But I had barely got to the doorway to give her a shout when the phone started ringing.

'Alan...'

I tried to cheer her up: 'There's an awful lot of wind about', 'Hold tight and it'll all blow away', 'Geoffrey was past it by now, anyway.'

I said, with suitable preface, that I would never seek to tell her who she should employ or why; but that if she could find something for 'Tim' to do...

'Tim who?' (thinking, I suppose, that I wanted her to bring someone called Tim into the Cabinet. Blast, blast. Too oblique. Never works with her.)

'Renton. You really ought to make Tristan your Chief Whip.'

A very long silence. I almost said 'hullo', but didn't.

'Oh but he's enjoying his present job so much ... '

I don't think she realises what a jam she's in. It's the Bunker syndrome. Everyone round you is clicking their heels. The saluting sentries have highly polished boots and beautifully creased uniforms. But out there at the Front it's all disintegrating. The soldiers are starving in tatters and makeshift bandages. Whole units are mutinous and in flight.

Saltwood   *Sunday, 11 November*

Back from Plymouth with what is, by tradition, the nastiest weekend of the year behind me. The Constituency engagements are dense and unyielding. The surgery is always particularly crowded and irksome. I invariably have a cold, often flu, and the Remembrance ceremonies on the Hoe drag and chill. New, and unwelcome, ecumenical balls caused the service to grate. Some nameless mystic read out words, unintelligible, from an unknown text. Drenching rain.

I had no time even to open a newspaper. But now I see that they are all packed with Heseltinia. Plugs of one kind or another. Some, like the *Mail on Sunday* (who had a heavy flirtation with David Owen at one point, I seem to recall), have quite openly changed sides. Every editor is uneasy. In the woodwork stir all those who have lived for the day when they could emerge and have a gloat without fear of retribution.

It looks to me as if Michael is going to get forced into a position, whether he likes it or not, when he'll have to stand. He's cunning and single-minded, yes. But he's also a bit, well, *dyslexic*. Galvanised, jerky movements. On the only two occasions when I have had anything to do with him on matters of policy, I recollect him getting into a great state.

When I was at Employment the question arose of whether a second frigate should be built at Cammell Laird, or at Swan Hunter. Michael has this infatuation with Liverpool, Merseyside, and it was all bound up with him showing his mettle to the crowd. He gabbled over the phone, was wild-eyed in the lobbies. Apparently threatened to resign. Why not? Get lost, she should have said, *then* give the contract to Cammells.

The second time was, of course, Westlands. I only spoke to him twice, something to do with Bristow's new fleet, quite marginal really, and found him almost off his head with rage and – to my mind – persecution mania.

Ministry of Defence   *Monday, 12 November*

I couldn't concentrate, and strolled over to the House. We are on the verge of great events. Wild rumours are circulating about the leadership 'contest' for which nominations close on Thursday. Today's favourite is that there just won't *be* a contest this year.

'Too close to the Election, old boy. Frozen.'

This has to be balls.

The Whips have totally clammed up. A bad sign. Already they have gone into 'neutral' mode. Secret policemen burning the old files, ready to serve.

The ballot would, should, be on Tuesday of next week. Only eight days to go and I have a dreadful feeling – not all the time, but in waves – that Heseltine will stand, and that he will win. I haven't communicated this to anyone. No one at all. But I wish Ian was alive.

House of Commons   *Tuesday, 13 November*

The Party is virtually out of control. Mutinous. People are not turning up for divisions. Dissidents get bolder and bolder with their little off-the-cuff TV slotettes. Code is abandoned. Discipline is breaking up. Geoffrey will make his resignation speech this afternoon, and apparently the entire text is the work of Elspeth. Received wisdom is that this will finally tear the whole thing wide open.

But why should it? Who gives a toss for the old

dormouse? Yet I suppose on the Berkeleian principle, if everyone thinks something is important, then it is important.

After Ministers this morning I signalled Andrew MacKay[26] to come into my room. He is so shrewd, he really knows the Party as well as any Whip. Why has he twice refused an invitation to join the Office?

We agreed that the situation is serious, very serious. It's the arithmetic that looks so nasty. There is this *bolus* of wankers, mainly in the North, who are fearful of losing their seats, and will try anything. Elizabeth Peacock:[27] 'We can't be any worse off than what (sic) we are.' Add this to Michael's own claque, itself at least fifty because adhering to it is the whole *Salon des Refusés*, plus all those like Charlie Morrison who have always loathed her, and before you know where you are you're dam' close to 150. Then, there is the considerable body of the soft optioneers, the abstentions. 'An honourable protest.' Crap on every side.

What a lot of people don't realise is that if we get a bad result, closeish figures, she will be hamstrung.

One can write Hugo Young, Peter Jenkins, Robin Oakley,[28] all those who've been waiting for this moment,

[26]Andrew MacKay, MP for Berkshire East since 1983. PPS to Tom King.
[27]Elizabeth Peacock, MP for Batley and Spen since 1983.
[28]Columnists Hugo Young (*Guardian*) and Peter Jenkins (*Independent*); Robin Oakley (Political Editor, *The Times*).

off the top of one's head. Broaden the Government; must think very long and hard about policy; Heseltine must enter the Cabinet; 'effectively Number Two'; the death-knell of Thatcherism – the clichés, leavened by spite, will roll.

At mid-day I had a meeting with Peter Levene. He told me that at the Lord Mayor's banquet last night she was greeted with virtually complete silence. She started punchily, then got flatter and flatter. I've seen her do this in the past. If the punchy bits don't get them going she reverts to text, and only rarely (Conference being one of the exceptions) are her texts any good.

We are at present in a state where any news, however slight and tenuous, spreads like wildfire if it is damaging. The effect is cumulative, and reinforces doubters, sceptics who need an excuse for transferring loyalties. 'She's virtually lost all support outside, you know . . .'

I change my own mind by the hour. In some ways it would be better for her to go completely than to hang on mutilated, forced to take in a Trojan Horse. But she has not got the nature to make a withdrawal to Colombey, and for that course it is now really too late. We're down to ensuring that Heseltine doesn't win in a stampede. And Douglas, who could play a role here, is deeply reluctant.

Later

I forced my way along the Minister of State's bench, stopping two places short of Janet [Fookes], who always sits, massively, in the camera-hogging spot just behind the

PM. The House was very full indeed, with much chattering and giggling from recusants. The loyalists are glum, and apprehensive.

From the moment he rose to his feet Geoffrey got into it. He was personally wounding – to a far greater extent than mere policy differences would justify. Elspeth's hand in every line.

All those Cabinets (seven *hundred* he said) when the Lady had lashed and basted him (there too, it must be admitted, more savagely than could be explained by nuances of attitude. But it was to a smaller audience and did not, I think, start until about three years ago). In his mind he will also have been carrying the brutal briefing on the 'non-existent' role of Deputy Prime Minister, the messing-around over the houses. It all seethed and bubbled in the cauldron.

The Labour benches loved it. Grinning from ear to ear they 'Oooh'd' and 'Aaah'd' dead on cue. At one point he illustrated his sense of betrayal with some cricketing analogy, being 'sent in to bat for Britain... only to find that before the game the bats have been broken by the team captain'. Everyone gasped and I looked round to catch Jonathan's eye. He had that special incredulous look he occasionally gets, mouth open.

Geoffrey ended his speech with an ominous, and strange, sentence: 'I have done what I believe to be right for my Party and for my Country.' (They all say that.) 'The time has come for others to consider *their own response* to the tragic conflict of loyalties with which I myself have wrestled for perhaps too long.'

Afterwards a lot of people, semi-traumatised, didn't want to talk about it. The atmosphere was light-headed, almost.

I spoke with Norman Lamont. He very naively ('I can see *you* weren't at Eton,' I said) questioned whether any member of the Government – not Cabinet, *Government* – could vote against her on the first ballot. 'Quite monstrously disloyal,' etc.

Afterwards I thought maybe it was a plant. You can't trust anyone at present.

We were joined by Tebbit. Wildish and gaunt he seemed. He mouthed a bit about a special role he was going to play; he had been in close touch with Peter M., and so on. Interestingly, he said we must *not* go for a compromise candidate. We must fight all the way, to the death.

This appeals to me. Leonidas at Thermopylae. But we don't win. It's the end of me. I came in with her. I go out with her.

House of Commons   *Wednesday, 14 November*

A curious state of limbo. Briefly, and unaccountably, the House has gone quiet. Many are leaving early for their constituencies to take the temperature.

The papers are terrible. The Lady is said to be 'foundering'; 'holed below the waterline'; 'stabbed'; 'bowled middle stump', and similar far from original metaphors. Much worse than Westland. There are even rumours (in the press, I can find no trace of them in the corridors so it may be a plant by Mates or Hampson[29]) that Cranley Onslow is going to advise her not even to *contest* the election.

Perfectly ridiculous. No one seems to have given a thought to the constitutional implications, still less the international. How can a narrow caucus in a singular political party unseat a Prime Minister just because it calculates that it may improve its election prospects thereby?

Tristan rang from his car. He's driving in from Heathrow, just back from some pointless and diverting voyage when he should be tirelessly cigaretting at the very centre of things here. Counting and calculating and ordering our deployment. Naturally he was *very* against NT's idea of a 'last stand'. He thinks he can fudge up a solution that will keep H out.

'Of course,' I said. 'If it works.'

'It's got to fucking work,' he answered.

Exciting, but unnerving, times.

---

[29]Dr Keith Hampson, MP for Leeds North-West since 1983 (Ripon 1974–83). PPS to Michael Heseltine, 1979–84. Before becoming an MP he was a personal assistant to Edward Heath in the 1966 and 1970 General Elections.

Saltwood   *Saturday, 17 November*

I have been listless and depressed most of the day, with
ill-at-ease tummy. Perhaps I drank too much in
Denmark.[30] But it was mainly Schnapps. Poisoned on
the aircraft, more likely. The papers are terrible. Only
exceptions being the leader of the *Daily Telegraph*, and
Paul Johnson.

Everything else is tipping Heseltine. Bandwagon. And
the five o'clock news was even worse. Heseltine doing
this, doing that; going down (or up) escalators; leaving
(or arriving at) his house. And all the time with that
uneasy, almost Wilsonian smirk. But among Conservatives
in the country she still has majority support. Alison, who
is sensible, remains a fervent fan. 'What *are* you all doing?'

The Lady herself is away, out of the country. It's absolute
madness. There is no Party mileage whatever in being at
the Paris summit. It just makes her seem snooty and
remote. And who's running the campaign? Who's doing
the canvassing? Who's putting the pressure on?

I became more and more dejected, decided to telephone
Tristan. He attempted to calm me, said that Peter Morrison was in charge of collating the votes, that he was
calmly confident. But when pressed Tristan shared
my scepticism as to whether this was really the true
picture.

[30] AC had been in Copenhagen for an IEPG meeting.

He launched into some dissertation as to how Douglas Hurd (who will be in Paris with the PM, about to go into a Banquet – shades of Potsdam) and John Major (who will – for God's sake – be in *hospital*, having just had four teeth taken out) will speak to each other in that first critical hour between 6 and 7 p.m. on Tuesday and, it is to be hoped, settle what should happen next.

I don't like the sound of this. It will be Halifax, Churchill and George VI, and they may decide who runs. In which case, *passim* Halifax, Douglas will probably stand aside. We're then left with John Major who, being calm and sensible, is infinitely preferable to that dreadful charlatan, H. But John is virtually unknown, too vulnerable to the subtle charge of 'not yet ready for it'.

He has personal handicaps, not of his own making. The product, indeed of his virtues. He's not at all *flash*, and a lot of colleagues think it's flash that we need at the moment. And he's not classy, which doesn't worry me in the slightest, but worse, he doesn't (like Mrs T.) even *aspire* to be classy.

Pinkish toffs like Ian [Gilmour] and Charlie [Morrison], having suffered, for ten years, submission to their social inferior see in Michael an arriviste, certainly, who can't shoot straight and in Jopling's damning phrase 'bought all his own furniture', but one who at any rate seeks the cachet. While all the nouves in the Party think he (Michael) is the real thing.

'Look,' I said. 'All these arguments are being tossed

around on the assumption that we have to go to a second ballot.'

'That's right, Baby.' (A strange affectation of Tristan's, calling me 'Baby'. I don't mind, but I do know from experience that it usually presages some piece of news which I am not going to like.)

An appalling thought struck me. Michael couldn't actually *win* first time round, could he? I put the question convolutedly. 'Do you think it more likely than not that he won't get a majority in the first ballot?'

'Yes.'

'Do you put the odds on this happening at worse than (longish pause) sixty per cent?'

'No.'

This is terrible. He's barely worse than evens.

Did I start gabbling? I don't remember. Tristan cut through it saying if there was any 'uncertainty' (good neutral word for the tapes) a group of us are to meet at Catherine Place after the 10 p.m. vote that evening.

I remain deeply anxious that The Establishment simply hasn't got the machinery, or the people, in place to operate effectively in that very narrow timescale.

I went down to the Winter Office, and drew up a little table showing the three alternatives. There are only three, none of them other than bad, though in varying degree, for me.

1) The PM survives, but maimed. The wind-down

period, perhaps to a Gentlemen's Coup in the spring. This is the best one can hope for, and would at least give me time to make some plans. I suppose it is just possible, by a combination of luck and circumstance such as she has enjoyed in the past, for her to make a gargantuan effort of 'projection', dump the Poll Tax, win the war, call a khaki election at once (it'd be nearly four years, after all) and once again be mother of her people. Certainly that is what I would advise. But good though she is, she's not in the shape of 1983, or even 1986 when she routed them over Westland.

2) It's A.N. Other, after a messy second ballot. Either Douglas or John Major would keep me, I'm pretty sure. Fun to watch a new administration getting the feel of things, but I would no longer be on the inner loop.

3) MH wins. Sudden Death. He might even have time to strike me off the PC list. Would anyone else refuse to serve? Cecil [Parkinson], I would think. Micky Forsyth and Eric Forth[31] certainly ought to. Peter Lilley[32] and the rest would just cower until he sacked them.

That's Politics (Baby).

[31] Michael Forsyth, MP for Stirling since 1983. Minister of State, Scottish Office, since 1990. Eric Forth, MP for Mid-Worcestershire since 1983. Parliamentary Under-Secretary, Employment.
[32] Peter Lilley, MP for St Albans since 1983. Financial Secretary at Treasury.

House of Commons   *Monday, 19 November*

The whole house is in ferment. Little groups, conclaves everywhere. Only in the dining room does some convention seem to have grown up (I presume because no one trusts their dining companions) that we don't talk 'shop'.

'Made your Christmas plans yet?' All that balls. God, the dining room is boring these days, even worse than Pratts'. Big, slow, buffers 'measuring their words' oh-so-firmly; or creepy little narks talking straight out of *Conservative News*.

But in the corridors it is all furtive whispering and glancing over shoulders. The institutional confidence (seen at its most obvious in those who have served a prison term, and which I first noticed in my early days on Warren Street[33]), that special grimacing style of speech out of the corner of the mouth, eyes focusing in another direction, is now it seems the only way of communicating.

Most people are interested – not so much in the result, as in knowing what the result will be in advance, in order to make their own 'dispositions'. To ingratiate oneself with the new regime – *a* new regime, I should say, because the outcome is by no means certain – even as little as a week before it is installed, looks better than joining the

---

[33]AC worked as a dealer's runner in Warren Street (at that time the focus of the trade market in used cars) for several months after coming down from Oxford.

stampede afterwards. The issue, which can be discussed semi-respectably, is who is most likely to deliver victory at the General Election? But it is packaging, conceals a great basket of bitterness, thwarted personal ambition, and vindictive glee. Talk of country, or loyalty, is dismissed as 'histrionics'.

And there is a strange feeling abroad. Even if the Lady wins – and here I am writing 'even if', pull yourself together Clark, say 'even after she's won' – there will be no escaping the fact that at least one hundred and fifty of her parliamentary colleagues will have rejected her leadership. That's a big chunk. Some people, particularly those who pose as Party Elders, like Tony Grant,[34] are intimating that it might be 'better' if, faced with so blatant a show of No Confidence, she decided to 'heal' the Party by announcing her intention to stand down at a given date (i.e., become a lame duck which the Labour Party could taunt and torment on every occasion, and a busted flush internationally).

And as the savour of a Heseltine victory starts to pervade the crannies and cupboards and committee rooms, so more and more people are 'coming out'. 'Oh, I don't think he'd be so bad, really...' 'He's got such a wide *appeal*.' 'My people just love him, I must say...' 'I know what you

---

[34]Sir Anthony Grant, MP for Cambridgeshire South-West since 1983 (Harrow Central, 1964–83).

mean, but he'd be so good at dealing with...' (fill in particular problem as appropriate).

Most conspicuous in canvassing are Hampson (loonily) Mates (gruffly) and Bill Powell[35] (persuasively). Michael himself is quite shameless in offering all and sundry what they have always wanted. For example, he would probably have got Paul's support anyway, but 'sealed' it with an assurance that Paul would be Speaker in the next House; Soames fell straight away for the 'your talents are long overdue for recognition' line, as did little Nelson[36] and Rhodes James ('you've been treated abominably').

Michael stands in the centre of the Members' lobby, virtually challenging people to wish him good luck. He gives snap 'updates' to journalists, and greets suppliants who are brought along for a short audience by his team. The heavier targets he sees in his room. The Cabinet play their cards close to the chest, although Mellor,[37] apparently, speaks to Michael twice a day on the telephone. Some, like Kenneth Clarke,[38] want her out so badly that they don't need even to blink. And I would guess that there are a fair coterie of Ministers of State and Parly Secs

[35]William Powell, MP for Corby since 1983.
[36]Anthony Nelson, MP for Chichester since 1974.
[37]David Mellor, Minister of State, Home Office, since 1989.
[38]Health Secretary since 1988.

like Sainsbury and Trippier[39] who feel uneasy with the Lady and like the idea of a change.

At the top of the ministerial staircase I ran into G-J. He was bubbling with suppressed excitement. I don't think he actually wants 'Hezzy' as he (spastically) calls him, to win. It would be disruptive of the Blue Chip long-term plan. But he's high on the whole thing.

Tristan said, 'Of course every member of the Cabinet will vote for the Prime Minister in the first round.' Like hell they will.

I said to him, hoping he'd deny it, 'One cannot actually exclude the possibility that Heseltine will score more votes than her on the first ballot.'

'No, I'm afraid one can't.'

'Can one, even, be completely sure that he will not get both the largest total and the necessary margin to win without a second ballot?'

'No, I'm afraid one can't.'

This was really chilling. Apocalypse. Because time is horrendously tight if we have to organise an alternative candidate. Four working days and a weekend. But if Michael scoops it in one gulp then that is the end of everything.

---

[39]Tim Sainsbury, MP for Hove since 1973, Parliamentary Secretary, Foreign Office. David Trippier, MP for Rossendale since 1979. Minister of State, Department of Environment, since 1989.

Maddeningly, I had to return to the Department. Meetings, and an official lunch. Scandinavians.

'I assume that there is no likelihood of Mrs Thatcher being defeated for the position of Prime Minister?'

'Oh no. None whatever. It's just one of these quaint traditions we have in the Conservative Party.'

But the encounter made me realise the enormity of what we're doing – *changing the Prime Minister* – but without any electoral authority so to do. I thought I'd have a talk to Peter,[40] although he doesn't encourage it, and I cancelled my early afternoon engagements and went back over to the House.

I listened outside the door. Silence. I knocked softly, then tried the handle. He was asleep, snoring lightly, in the leather armchair, with his feet resting on the desk.

Drake playing bowls before the Armada and all that, but I didn't like it. This was ten minutes past three in the afternoon of the most critical day of the whole election. I spoke sharply to him. 'Peter.'

He was bleary.

'I'm sorry to butt in, but I'm really getting a bit worried about the way things are going.'

'Quite all right, old boy, relax.'

'I'm just hearing bad reactions around the place from people where I wouldn't expect it.'

[40]Peter Morrison was in charge of Mrs Thatcher's campaign.

'Look, do you think I'd be like this if I wasn't entirely confident?'

'What's the arithmetic look like?'

'Tight-ish, but OK.'

'Well, what?'

'I've got Michael on 115. It could be 124, at the worst.'

'Look, Peter, I don't think people are being straight with you.'

'I have my ways of checking.'

'Paul?'

'I know about Paul.'

'The Wintertons?'[41]

'The Wintertons, funnily enough, I've got down as "Don't Know's".'

'What the fuck do you mean, "*Don't Know*"? This isn't a fucking street canvas. It's a two-horse race, and each vote affects the relative score by two, unless it's an abstention.'

'Actually, I think there could be quite a few abstentions.'

'Don't you think we should be out there twisting arms?'

'No point. In fact it could be counter-productive. I've got a theory about this. I think some people may abstain on the first ballot in order to give Margaret a fright, then rally to her on the second.' (Balls, I thought, but didn't say.)

'What about the '92? They're completely rotten.

---

[41]Nick Winterton, MP for Macclesfield since 1971, and his wife Ann, MP for Congleton since 1983.

They've got a meeting at six. Are you going?'

'No point. But I think *you* should.'

In deep gloom I walked back down Speaker's corridor. It can't really be as bad as this can it? I mean there is absolutely no oomph in her campaign *whatsoever*. Peter is useless, far worse than I thought. When he was pairing Whip he was unpopular, but at least he was crisp. Now he's sozzled. There isn't a single person working for her who cuts any ice at all. I know it's better to be feared than loved. But these people aren't either. And she's in Paris. '*Où est la masse de manoeuvre? -Aucune.*'

I went into the members' tea room. The long table was crowded with Margaret supporters, all nonentities except for Tebbit who was cheering people up. Much shouting and laughter. Blustering reassurance. Norman was saying how unthinkable it was to consider dismissing a Prime Minister during a critical international conference. 'Like Potsdam in 1945,' I said. No one paid any attention. If they heard they didn't, or affected not to, understand the allusion.

The crowd thinned out a little and when he got up Norman said that he wanted a word. We went into the Aye lobby and sat at that round table in the centre with all the stationery on it.

'Well ... ?'

'It's filthy,' I said.

'It could be close. Very close.'

I agreed, '*Fucking* close.'

'If it's like that do you think she should stand in the second ballot?'

I simply don't know the answer to this. Governing would be very difficult with half the Party against her. She might have to make 'concessions' to the left. I asked Norman if he thought she would have to bring Heseltine into the Cabinet?

'She'd certainly be under a lot of pressure to do so.'

'Renton.'

'Yeah.'

I said that the key tactic was to get Chris Patten to stand, and draw off the left vote. At least the hard left vote, Charlie Morrison, Bob Hicks,[42] all the wankers. Norman said, 'And Ken Clarke.' I told him no, if you have too many candidates people just get in a muddle and Heseltine walks through them, just as she did in 1975. Norman said that a lot of people now regarded Michael as a *right*-wing candidate anyway.

'Well, we know different.'

'Too true.'

Norman said, 'If it's open season, I'm dam' well going to put my name in. The right must have a candidate they can vote for.'

'You'd lose.'

'It's likely I would, but at least we'd know our strength.

[42]Robert Hicks, MP for Cornwall South-East since 1983 (Bodmin, 1970-March 1974; October 1974–83).

That could be useful in a changed situation.'

'Look, Norman, we want to put additional names in to reduce *his* total, not ours. I don't think Heseltine has that big a personal vote. It's just an anti-Margaret coalition.'

I could see he was thoughtful. But he didn't want to prolong the conversation, which we were conducting in tones just above a whisper, though still arousing the curious attention of passers-by.

Raising his voice Norman said, 'Well, this time tomorrow everything will be settled,' and gave one of his graveyard cackles.

The '92 meeting was in one of those low-ceilinged rooms on the upper committee room corridor. The mood was tetchy, and apprehensive. There was a kind of fiction running from several (Jill Knight, for example, shockingly), just as Norman had foreseen, that 'Michael' – as defectors call him (supporters of the Prime Minister always refer to him as 'Heseltine'; and this is quite a useful subliminal indicator of how the speaker is going to vote when he or she is being deliberately or defensively opaque) – was 'really' on the right.

The trouble with this club, to which I was elected almost as soon as I arrived here, but with which I have never really felt comfortable, is that it personifies in extreme form two characteristics found in the majority of MPs – stupidity and egomania. It is only the shrewd and subtle guidance of George Gardiner[43] that has prevented them becoming a laughing stock in recent years. But such integrity as they might originally have possessed has been eroded by the inclusion of many from marginal seats. None are quite as awful as Elizabeth Peacock, who spoke squatly and fatly against Margaret – why bother, she won't be here in the next Parliament anyway[44] – but most are concerned solely with saving their own skins. I spoke loyally and, should have been movingly, of our debt of loyalty to the PM. But there was a hint of what's-she-ever-done-for-us from the audience and with some justification, so few ministerial appointments having come out of the '92. I tried to make their flesh creep with what Michael would do, got only a subdued ritual cheer when I said Margaret is undefeated, and never will be defeated either in the Country or in this House of Commons. I'm not particularly popular with that lot. They think I'm 'snooty'. Perhaps my boredom threshold shows. But in the ballot tomorrow I'd say they will divide no better than 60/40.

After dinner I had a word with Norman Lamont. He'd just come back from somewhere-or-other. 'I don't like the smell,' he kept saying. 'There's a bad smell to the whole

---

[43]Sir George Gardiner, MP for Reigate since 1974. Secretary of '92.
[44]In fact the prediction by AC was in the result shown to be defective. In the 1992 General Election she retained her seat by a margin of 1408.

place.' He's right, of course. It's the smell of decay. It's affecting everything, the badge messengers, the police, the drivers. Something nasty is going to happen.

I write this very late, and I am very tired. Perhaps I'm just needlessly depressed. I'd ring the Lady if I could, but she's at a banquet. She's not even coming back for the ballot. Lovely and haughty.

Albany   *Tuesday, 20 November*

The afternoon hung interminably. Labour MPs were everywhere, ghoulish and heavy-handed with their jokes. Our fellows seemed all to be in hiding.

As is my style at all 'counts' I went up to the committee floor very late. A huge crowd in the corridor. The entire lobby, TV teams from all over the world. (How did they get in, pray – all part of the general breakdown of order and discipline which is licking, like stubble fire, at everything in the Palace these last two days.)

There was, inevitably, a balls-up over the figures. We, the Tory MPs, packed tight and hot and jumpily joking to each other in the committee room, did not (a monstrous error by Cranley Onslow, for which he will pay at the next election[45]) get the figures first. We heard a loud noise,

---

[45]The error was to give the voting figures to the press first. At the next election for the chairmanship of the 1922 Committee Onslow was defeated by Sir Marcus Fox.

something between a gasp and a cheer, from outside the door, as the journalists digested first the closeness of the result, then the killer element – that there had under the rules to be a second ballot.

Four votes, that was all there was in it. I get so cross when I remember Peter Morrison asleep in his office. For want of a nail a kingdom was lost.

I dined with Jonathan Aitken and Nick Budgen. Bruce was at the table. To my amazement they were all confident. 'She'll wipe the floor with him next time round.' 'The abstainers will all come in.' 'You don't understand, Alan, all those people who wanted to give her a fright, they'll support her now she's up against it.'

How can people get things so wrong?

Perhaps there was a lot of this kind of muddled thinking around before the ballot. But that's historic. She's a loser, now. Doomed.

I hardly bothered to argue with them. I suppose my dejection was infectious because, by the coffee, we were all silent. Save Bruce who, although jobless, is going to shut himself away and do a Randolph,[46] an instant book on the leadership campaign.

At the ten o'clock vote Tristan found me in the lobby,

[46]In 1963 Randolph Churchill wrote *The Fight for the Tory Leadership: A Contemporary Chronicle* (Heinemann), an account of the way in which the Conservative Party selected Lord Home as leader following the resignation of Harold Macmillan.

pulled me into the window bay by the writing table. 'We're meeting at my house, straight after this.'

'Who's "we"?'

'Oh just a few mates; *Chris* and people. We need to talk through the next steps.'

'How do you mean?'

'Ways of supporting the Prime Minister.'

But he wouldn't accede to any of my suggestions; Aitken, Maude, David Davis[47] or Lilley, in that order. Even Andrew MacKay (not obviously of the right, as were the others) caused Tristan to pull a long face.

'We're all friends. It's a very small gathering, we all know each other and can speak freely...'

As soon as I walked into the room it was apparent why no one else from the right had been allowed in. 'Blue-Chips' wall-to-wall. Five Cabinet Ministers. Rifkind, who was the most dominant, and effective; C. Patten, also good but (relatively) taciturn; Newton, and Waldegrave.

Waldegrave was sympathetic, in a relaxed, jokey way. The only person to say what a personal tragedy it was for her, how she was still of a different dimension to all the others. Lamont was there, stood throughout, Mephis-tophelean in his black tie. He shocked me by saying at the

---

[47]Francis Maude, MP for Warwickshire South, Minister of State, Foreign Office; David Davis, MP for Boothferry since 1987. PPS to Eric Forth.

outset that he could conceive of Michael as being quite an 'effective', *tolerable* (sic) Prime Minister.

Patten said, 'Well, he's not mad, is he? I mean after you've had a meal with him you don't get up from the table and think, that fellow was mad, do you?'

There were three Ministers of State in the room, besides myself, Hogg and John Patten. Tim Yeo[48] was there 'representing' Hurd, whose PPS he is, but stayed silent.

Douglas Hogg piped up, 'I think any one of us could serve under him [Michael].' And there was a sort of cautious mumble of assent. What I assume he meant, of course, was, 'I don't think anyone in this room is likely to be sacked – so we can all enjoy ourselves.' Mutual preening took place.

I said it wasn't quite as easy as that. What we had to ensure was that the person who replaces her is the one most likely to win the Election.

'All right, then, Al; what do you think?'

Michael was unreliable, I argued. Any electoral capital he brought would soon be expended. What we needed now was a Baldwin, someone to reassure rather than stimulate. I expanded, people were nodding. But when I said Tom King, Chris Patten laughed aloud. And John P., taking his cue, said, 'I presume you're joking.'

Tristan said, 'Come on, Al, you'll have to do better than that.'

[48]Tim Yeo, MP for Suffolk South since 1983.

Only Douglas Hogg, surprisingly, admitted that he saw the point.

I had one more go. I did *not* say that Tom was Willie's choice as well as mine. That might have generated a class backlash. But I dwelt on his overall departmental experience in Northern Ireland, how good he was on the stump, as I had often seen.

Yet as I was speaking it dawned on me that winning the Election was not uppermost in all their minds. They were, most of them, twenty years younger than me, carving out their own career prospects and wanting to identify with the new winner.

Not only was there no one of my generation, there was no one (although Richard, who is a Norfolk Squire, came in very much later) of my background. There was no one, except possibly Tris, who understands and loves the Tory Party for all its faults, knows it as an old whore that has been around for 400 years.

Young Turks. And Young Turks are bad news, unless there is some dilution. They all poke fun at Tom now. But if he became Prime Minister, assumed the authority, he could metamorphose and put them all in irons. The old Postman in Remarque's *All Quiet*...

Although I had been expecting Tristan to try and rig it for John Major, the concensus did in fact build up quite rapidly for Douglas. I remained doubtful. He is *too* much of an Establishment candidate.

Of course, this is a crisis for the Establishment, and they

have left it horrendously late to organise. But DH looks, speaks, moves, articulates as prototypical Establishment. I'm not sure the Party wants that. It's very risky, unless there is another candidate from the left who will peel off a tranche of Heseltine's total.

It is difficult. If we confine the contest to two candidates, the issues are starker. If there are more than two there will be some cross-transferring, but there remains a danger that Michael's core vote will be strong enough – just as she herself (opposed by the Establishment) was in 1975. Never mind the abstruse calculations according to the 'Rules', the third ballot is a foregone conclusion. Whoever gets the highest total next time, wins.

It was only when I got back here, at ten minutes to one a.m. that it dawned on me: at least five of the people in that room fancied themselves as 'New Generation' candidates, in the nearish future. They want Douglas, but *as a caretaker*. They're not quite ready, themselves. As we were breaking up one – it could have been William – actually said, 'If we put John in, he'll be there for twenty-five years.'

The really sickening thing, though, was the urgent and unanimous abandonment of the Lady. Except for William's little opening tribute, she was never mentioned again.

Albany   *Wednesday, 21 November*

This is going to be – politically – The Longest Day. I woke
very early, in spite of having gone to bed at twenty past
one, and with a restless energy matched only by that on
the February morning in 1986 when I knew that at last I
had escaped from the DE and was to be appointed Minister
for Trade. Yet today it is the exact reverse. Not only
my own prospects, but the whole edifice which we have
constructed around the Lady, are in ruins.

It's quite extraordinary. Fifteen years have gone by and
yet those very same people – Dykes, Charlie Morrison,
Tony Grant, Barney Hayhoe[49] – who have always hated
her and the values she stood for, are still around in the
lobbies, barely looking any different, grinning all over
their faces – 'At last we've got her.'

I can't think of a single anti-Thatcherite who has died
or receded throughout that entire period.

By 6.30 my tea was cold and I had read the papers. Still
an assumption, in some columns, that Michael will be
defeated in the second ballot – but by whom?

Always remember what she did in '75; all that shit
about now its 'really' going to be Willie, or Jim Prior,[50] or

[49]Hugh Dykes, MP for Harrow East since 1970. Sir Barney
Hayhoe, MP for Brentford since 1970.
[50]Jim Prior (Life Peer 1987). MP for Lowestoft, 1959–83
(Waveney 1983–7). A former Leader of the Commons.

you name it. The Party may be just entering on one of its periodic bouts of epilepsy.

I put a call through to Paris. They're one hour ahead, and I wanted to interrupt the pre-breakfast conference. Peter came on the line. I said I must have two minutes with her. Charles would have always put me through. So would Bernard. He gave me the usual runaround. Frightfully tied up just at this minute, try and fit it in before we go down to breakfast . . .

'Go *down* to? Don't you have it in the room?'

'There's a Working Breakfast.'

'With a lot of fucking foreigners, I suppose. I want to talk to her about last night.' I gave him a (selective) résumé of events at Catherine Place.

'I'll try and call you back.'

'When?'

'Well, within half an hour.'

'Peter, you will tell her I rang, won't you?'

'Yes, yes. Yes.'

'Because if you tell her, she will call me. And if she doesn't call me, I'll know it's because you haven't told her.'

High-pitched giggle. 'Don't worry. I'll tell her.' He won't though. Cunt.

Later
Ministry of Defence
No work is being done in Whitehall today, whatsoever.
My 'In'-tray is about an inch deep. I don't think a single
Minister in the Govt will be at his desk; or if he is, it will
be only so as to telephone to a colleague or to a journalist.
The civil servants (all of whom, down to Principal level, I
suspect, were terrified of the Lady) just can not believe
their eyes.

Yet still she won't return. There is talk of a 'fighting
statement' later. But this wastage of time in Paris is sheer
lunacy. Harold at Stamford Bridge.

It is the general sense of disintegration now affecting
everything, that is so damaging to her. Unless MH is
slaughtered in the final ballot – impossibly unlikely – she
herself is going to find it highly difficult to reassert her
authority, even if eventually she emerges as the victor.
Short, that is, of giving them the full coup-loser's treat-
ment – arrest, manacles, beaten up in the interrogation
room, shot while trying to escape. Real blood, in other
words. Fun, but a bit *Angolan*.

Before walking over to the House I called Andrew
MacKay into my room and we had a long talk about Tom.
Earlier, we had both lingered after Ministers and sounded
him.

Tom likes the idea, preened himself, straightened his
jacket; but he is cautious. He would need to be sure of at
least thirty votes to even 'put down a marker'. And in any

case, convention obliges that no member of the Cabinet puts his name forward while she is still standing. (I hear rumours that that pudgy puff-ball Kenneth Clarke is considering breaching this, but am keeping that in reserve.)

'Look,' I told him. 'If the Lady is doomed, our Number One priority is to find, and instal a leader who will win the next General Election. And we haven't got long. Who is best suited to do this?'

I told him that Heseltine would burn out very quickly. His rhetoric pleased Party Conference, but was less reliable in the national context. Anyway people are sick of passion, they want reassurance.

The only two figures who can do this are Tom and John Major. Douglas is now past it; is thought rightly or wrongly to be a buffer and a bureaucrat. John is more engaging than Tom in some ways, with a lovely grin, but seems really too youthful. There is no time to project him. Even in the House he is barely known, has never been seen under fire. Tom, on the other hand, does have gravitas. Also he's good on the stump, in small groups, canteens and so on.

Andrew was in broad agreement. But:

'Tom won't make a move while she's still in the field.'

'So what do we do?'

'I tell you what I'm doing, if she stands second time round – voting for Michael.'

I was appalled. Here was this good, intelligent man, tough and (in so far as it still means anything) right wing . . . More than any other experience this conversation has made me realise that she will lose, finally, head-to-head against Heseltine. But if she does stand again we are in a log-jam; the only people who will join in the contest are wankers like Clarke who are not worth twenty-five votes.

Andrew said that he would, very quietly, take soundings for Tom. The immediate priority is to find a way, tactfully and skilfully, to talk her out of standing a second time.

Now I must close this entry and walk over to the House.

House of Commons

I was greeted with the news that there had been an announcement. 'I fight, and I fight to win.' God alive!

Tebbit is holding an impromptu press conference in the Members' lobby.

Fifty feet away, down the tea-room corridor that mad ninny Hampson is dancing around on his tippy-toes calling out to passers-by, 'Tee-hee, she's standing. We've made it. We can't lose now, etc.'

I came back here, to my room. I kept the door open and an endless succession of visitors trooped in and out. No one seems to have any idea of what we should do. Her 'Campaign' is a shambles now. John Moore (who he?) is running around with bits of paper – 'draft statements' – asking people what they think. He seems to have a temporary HQ in Portillo's room, which is next door to mine. First I heard that Norman Fowler was going to take

charge; then John Wakeham. Or was it the other way
round? Gamelin's been sacked, Weygand is on the way out;
Pétain's in the wings. '*Où est la masse de manoeuvre? –
Aucune.*'

Every time I trawl the corridors I run into another batch
of chaps who say they're going to switch, or abstain,
or when-are-there-going-to-be-some-more-candidates-to-
choose-from? The only visitor who has made any real
sense is Francis Maude. He claims, forcefully, that John
Major has a better chance than we all realise. But John
won't make a move while the Lady remains in the field. 'I
must get to see her. Can you help?' Apparently Peter stands
sentinel, and is outside her door the whole time.

I have closed the door. These random conversations are
too discursive. Tomorrow is the last day for nominations.
I must clear my head.

1) If she fights head on, she loses.

2) Therefore, the opposition vote has got to be diluted
by a candidate from the left – preferably Patten, making
it triangular. Besides dilution, this has the advantage that
it will crack Cabinet 'solidarity' open and others may lose
their scruples. Therefore:

3) Try and talk Patten into standing. QED.

Archie Hamilton's just been in. Didn't make any sense.
One minute he says she 'could still' win; the next that
we've all 'had it'. I'm off now, upstairs.

Later
Kundan Restaurant
It is very late, and finally I have withdrawn here for a vegetable curry, and to write up the traumatic happenings of this evening.

I made first for Chris's room. On the way I passed her outer door and said to Peter that I must have a minute or so. He looked anxious, almost rattled, which he never does normally. 'I'll do my best. She's seeing every member of the Cabinet in turn...'

'Francis wants to see her too.'

'I'm doing my best.'

Chris wasn't in his room. The Secretary of State's corridor was deserted. Hushed, but you could feel the static.

The policeman by the lift said he was 'in with Mr Rifkind'.

I knocked and went in without waiting for an answer. Also in there, loathesomely conspiring, was little Kenneth Clarke. Her three great ill-wishers! Clarke wasn't friendly at all. If he'd said anything to me, I'd have answered 'Fuck you', so just as well.

Chris was quite amiable.

'How many votes she got at the moment?'

'It's a rout. She's down to ninety.'

'*Ninety*?'

'You've got to stand. You can't let Michael corner the left.'

He was diplomatic. A discussion was impossible. God

knows what they were talking about, but it stank. Never mind, I have sowed the seed; or watered what was already there.

I went down the stairs and rejoined the group outside her door. After a bit Peter said, 'I can just fit you in now – but only for a split second, mind.'

She looked calm, almost beautiful. 'Ah, Alan . . .'

'You're in a jam.'

'I know that.'

'They're all telling you not to stand, aren't they?'

'I'm going to stand. I have issued a statement.'

'That's wonderful. That's heroic. But the Party will let you down.'

'I am a fighter.'

'Fight, then. Fight right to the end, a third ballot if you need to. But you lose.'

There was quite a little pause.

'It'd be so terrible if Michael won. He would undo everything I have fought for.'

'But what a way to go! Unbeaten in three elections, never rejected by the people. Brought down by nonentities!'

'But Michael . . . as *Prime Minister*.'

'Who the fuck's Michael? No one. Nothing. He won't last six months. I doubt if he'd even win the Election. Your place in history is towering . . .'

Outside, people were doing that maddening trick of opening and shutting the door, at shorter and shorter intervals.

'Alan, it's been so good of you to come in and see me . . .'

Afterwards I felt empty. And cross. I had failed, but I didn't really know what I wanted, except for her still to be Prime Minister, and it wasn't going to work out.

I sat on the bench immediately behind the Speaker's chair, watching the coming and going. After a bit Tristan came and sat beside me. But he had little to say. What is there to say? She's still seeing visitors. Then, along came Edwina.

'Hullo, aren't you Edwina Currie?'[51]

'Now then, Alan, there's no need to be objectionable.'

'If that is who you are, I must congratulate you on the combination of loyalty and restraint that you have shown in going on television to announce your intention to vote against the Prime Minister in the Leadership Election.'

'Alan, I'm perfectly prepared to argue this through with you, if you'll listen.'

'Piss off.'

Which she did.

Tristan said, 'She's not a bad girl really.'

At half past eight I left to come over here. The archway exit from Speaker's Court was blocked by the PM's Jaguar. She had just taken her seat, and as the detective's door slammed the interior light went out and the car slid away. I realised with a shock that this was in all probability her

[51]Edwina Currie, MP for Derbyshire South since 1983.

last night as Prime Minister. I came in with her. I go out with her, and a terrible sadness envelops me – of unfinished duties and preoccupations; of dangers and injustices remaining, of the greed, timidity and short-sightedness of so many in public life.

Albany   *Thursday, 22 November*

Very early this morning the phone rang. It was Tristan.
  'She's going.'
  There will be an official announcement immediately after a short Cabinet, first thing. Then the race will be on. Apparently Douglas *and* John Major are going to stand. I said I thought it was crazy, Heseltine will go through between them. I could sense him shrugging. 'There you go.'
  Anyway, would I come over to his room at the Foreign Office and watch it from there?
  Afterwards, very *triste* and silent, I walked back to the MoD and sat in on a late (and unnecessary) Ministers' meeting. Tom told us that it had been 'awful'. She started to read a prepared statement to them, then broke down, and the text had to be finished by the Lord Chancellor.
  Listless, I drifted over to the House. I had a word with Charles, drafted a couple of valedictory passages for her speech[52] this afternoon, did I don't know how many impromptu TV bites.

[52]Not in fact used. Mrs Thatcher told AC that if she had, she would have broken down again.

Heseltine is meant to be coming to Plymouth tomorrow, for a fundraising dinner. I rang Judith,[53] told her we couldn't possibly allow him to use us as a platform to plug his own candidature. She only half agreed, so I immediately telephoned to the *Western Morning News* and told them that I had 'instructed' that the invitation be withdrawn. (Not unrich, considering I was not the host, and had long ago told everyone that I wanted nothing to do with it.)

I didn't think I could bear it, but curiosity drew me into the Chamber for the Lady's last performance. It would have been too macabre to have sat in my habitual place, next to her PPS, so I watched and listened first from behind the Chair, then from the Bar of the House. She was brilliant. Humorous, self-deprecating, swift and deadly in her argument and in her riposte. Even Dennis Skinner, her oldest adversary, was feeding her lines; and at one point Michael Carttiss[54] shouted, 'You could wipe the floor with the lot of 'em.'

Too bloody true. What is to become of her? Acclimatisation will be agony, because she is not of that philosophic turn of mind that would welcome a spell at Colombey. Can she just remain on the back benches? It will be hard. What happens when she starts to be 'missed', and the rose-

---

[53] Judith Roberts, Chairman of the Sutton Division.
[54] Michael Carttiss, MP for Great Yarmouth since 1983.

tinted spectacles are found in everyone's breast pocket?

This evening I had a strange, possibly a significant experience. There is a semi permanent prefab studio on College Green, where endless conclaves of MPs record their comments on the respective vices and virtues of the second-round candidates. Around it are many secondary groupings, each with a shoulder-held video and a very bright light, recording any, yes any, it seems, comment by any, yes, any one who is going past.

Emerging from this brilliantly lit pool into the darkness at its edge, I was accosted by a familiar figure who, being dazzled, I did not at first recognise.

'Hey, Alan, take a look at this.'

It was Bob Worcester.[55] He showed me a poll, the first to be run, asking how respondents would vote if (names) were leading the Tory Party. One of Michael's great hidden strengths has always been the huge margin which he had over Mrs Thatcher in this very context. To my amazement, I saw that John Major had already drawn level! And in one case was actually ahead, actually preferred not withstanding the *continuous* exposure which Michael has had these last two weeks.

'Christ, Bob, these have to be rogue figures.'

[55]Robert Worcester. Head of MORI, the opinion polls organisation.

Bob took umbrage. 'Look, Alan, we're MORI. We don't have "rogue" figures.'

This could be critically important. If John can break through here, he's won.

Not so many in the Party really want to vote Heseltine, for himself. Some do, and will, just to spite her. But the bulk of Michael's support comes from his so-called Election–winning powers. People have guilt about condoning what he did to Her. Once they have a real reason to do so, they'll abandon him.

Tomorrow's papers will tell us more. I am taking an early train to Plymouth to 'sound out' feeling (i.e., get cover for the way I cast my vote). But even if I can't get a single person in the town to tell me to vote for John Major, that's what I'm going to do.

In the Ruler of Oman's DC9   Wednesday, 28 November

I am winging my way out to the Gulf.[56] I am *not* a Minister, as Private Office were (unhealthily) eager to explain to me. So there will be no HE to greet me with his Union Jack bedecked Jaguar. I will have no status with dignitaries or administrators (like hell, I thought, just watch me). This is because, with a new PM, all ministerial appoint-

---

[56]The *Cercle*, an Atlanticist Society of right-wing dignitaries, largely compered by Julian Amery and Herr Franz-Joseph Bach, staged one or two conferences a year and this one was travelling to Oman at the hospitality of the Ruler.

ments lapse, revert to his gift, and have to be 'confirmed'.

It is pleasing to be at 35,000 feet, carving our route to the warm waters of the Arabian Gulf, while behind in Britain colleagues lick their wounds, or feel stale with anti-climax. Was it only last night that Jane and I watched Cranley, on the TV screen in Needham's office,[57] bellowing the figures, and then very shortly after, Michael conceded?

There was one strange, unscripted episode. Very late in the evening, after I had seen Jane off in the car, I was coming up that back staircase which leads from the transport office and comes out in the Members' lobby. At the last turn in the landing I heard the top door open in a rush and there, quite alone, wild-eyed and head to head stood Heseltine.

'Hullo Michael,' I said.

He made no answer, rushed past. He could say he had 'cut' me. But he was a zombie, shattered.

It was Mates who brought him the numbers. Must it not at that moment have been:

> A Great Hope fell.
> You heard no noise
> The Ruin was Within.[58]

[57]Richard Needham (Earl of Kilmorey, but does not use the title). MP for Wiltshire North since 1983 (Chippenham, 1979–83).
[58]Emily Dickinson.